Princess L.P. And Her Little Owl

By

K.D. MITCHELL

Available on Amazon markets

GG the owl

K. D. Mitchell

Available on Amazon markets

UNDER THE SEA
The Amazing Octopus

K.D. MITCHELL

Illustrator: Aleksandra Miasmatique

For Cartier

Cartier and his family,
often, went snorkeling in the sea, at a nearby coral reef.

Let's snorkel!

butterfly fish

butterfly fish

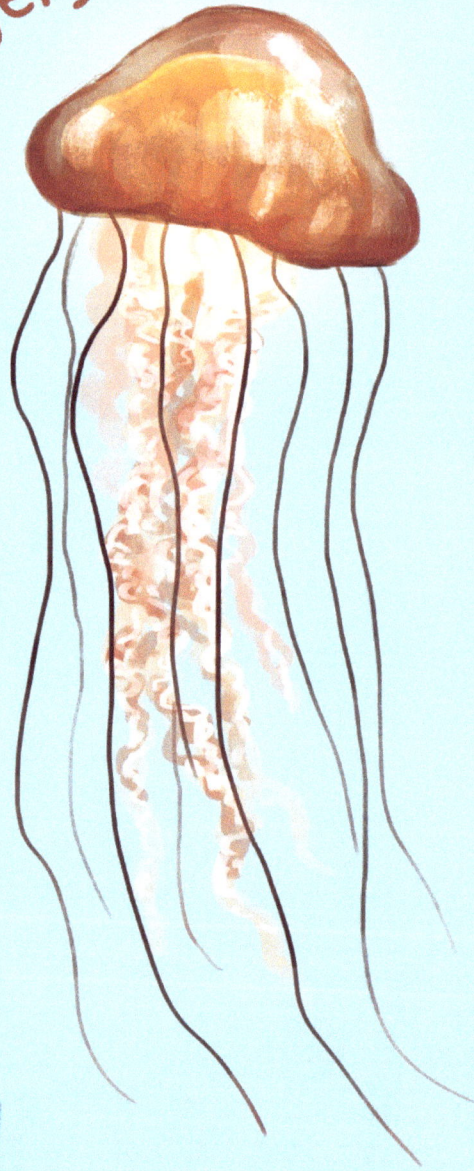

jelly fish

sea turtle

clownfish

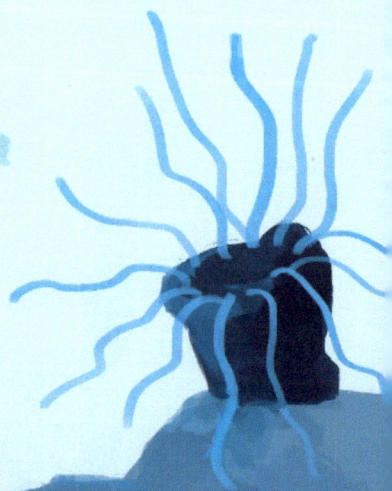

turkey fish

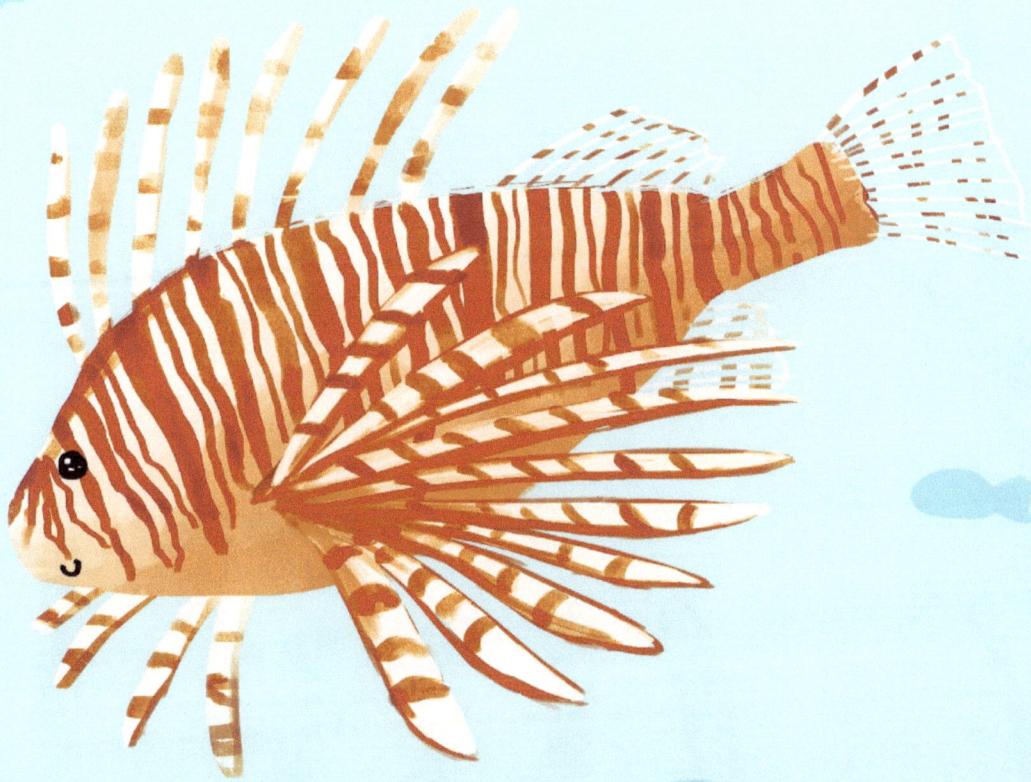

octopus

peacock fish

sea snail

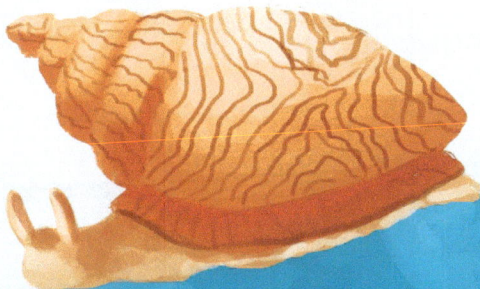

One day...

One day, while Cartier was watching a snail near the octopus cave, he felt a slight tickling, touching feeling on his hand and fingers. Looked down at his hand, he saw the octopus tentacles. They were feeling his hand and fingers. Cartier thought that it was funny and let it be until he had to come up for air. He had seen this octopus a few times.

Cartier likes to think that he has more friends than anyone in the whole wide world! Most cute, and gentle manner animals in the woods, many birds in the air, and many aquamarine animals are his friends.

Lately, his family spent quite a bit of time snorkeling. Cartier met new friends – beautiful fishes, star fish sea-dragons, sea-snails, sea-turtles, urchins, and many more – which were living in the great colorful coral reef - They've grown familiar with seeing him around, and Cartier never bothered them. He only watched them go about their lives. Few very friendly fish swam right up to him, and nibbled his fingers, or let him pet them.

stingray

parrotfish

crab

lobster

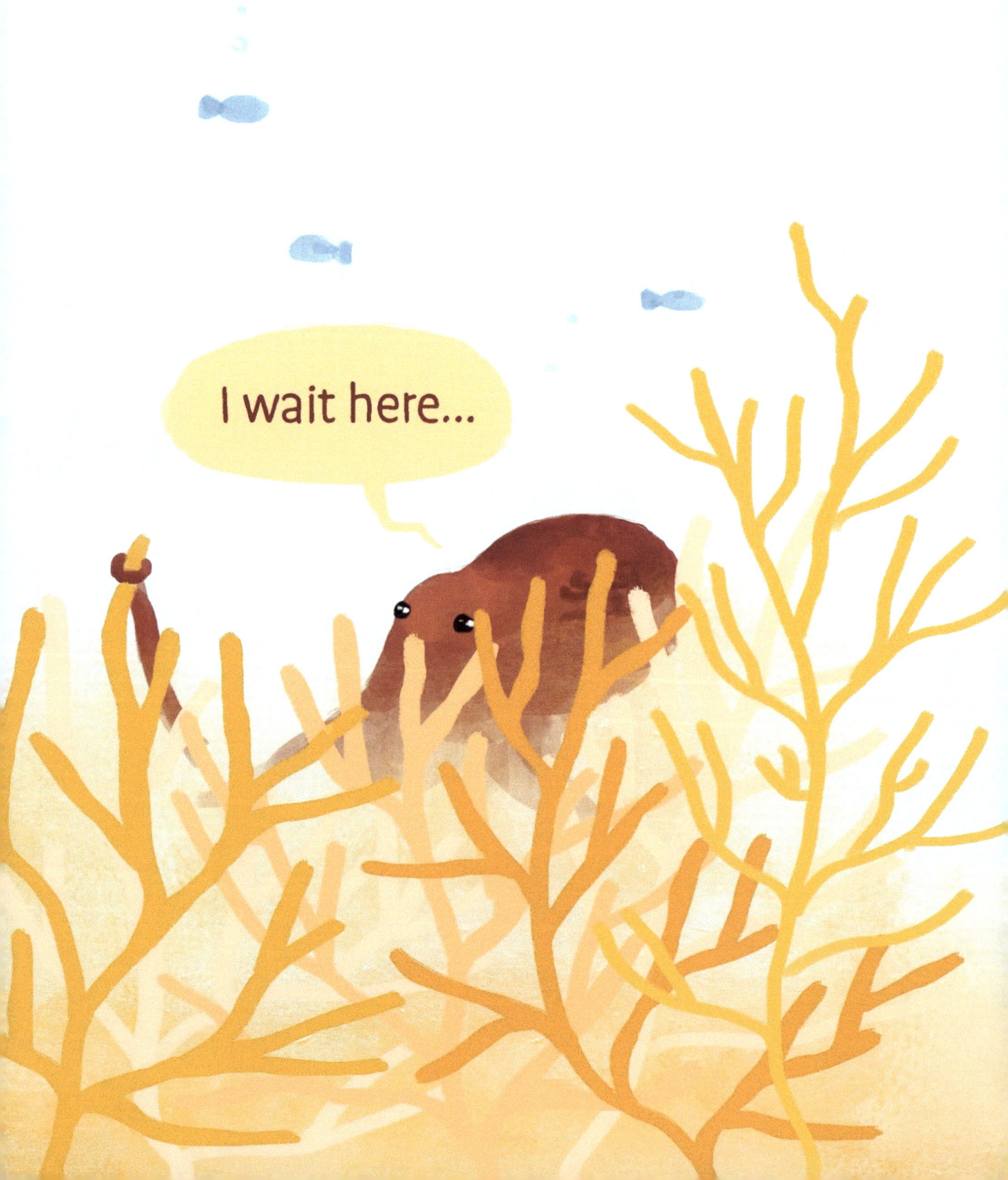
I wait here...

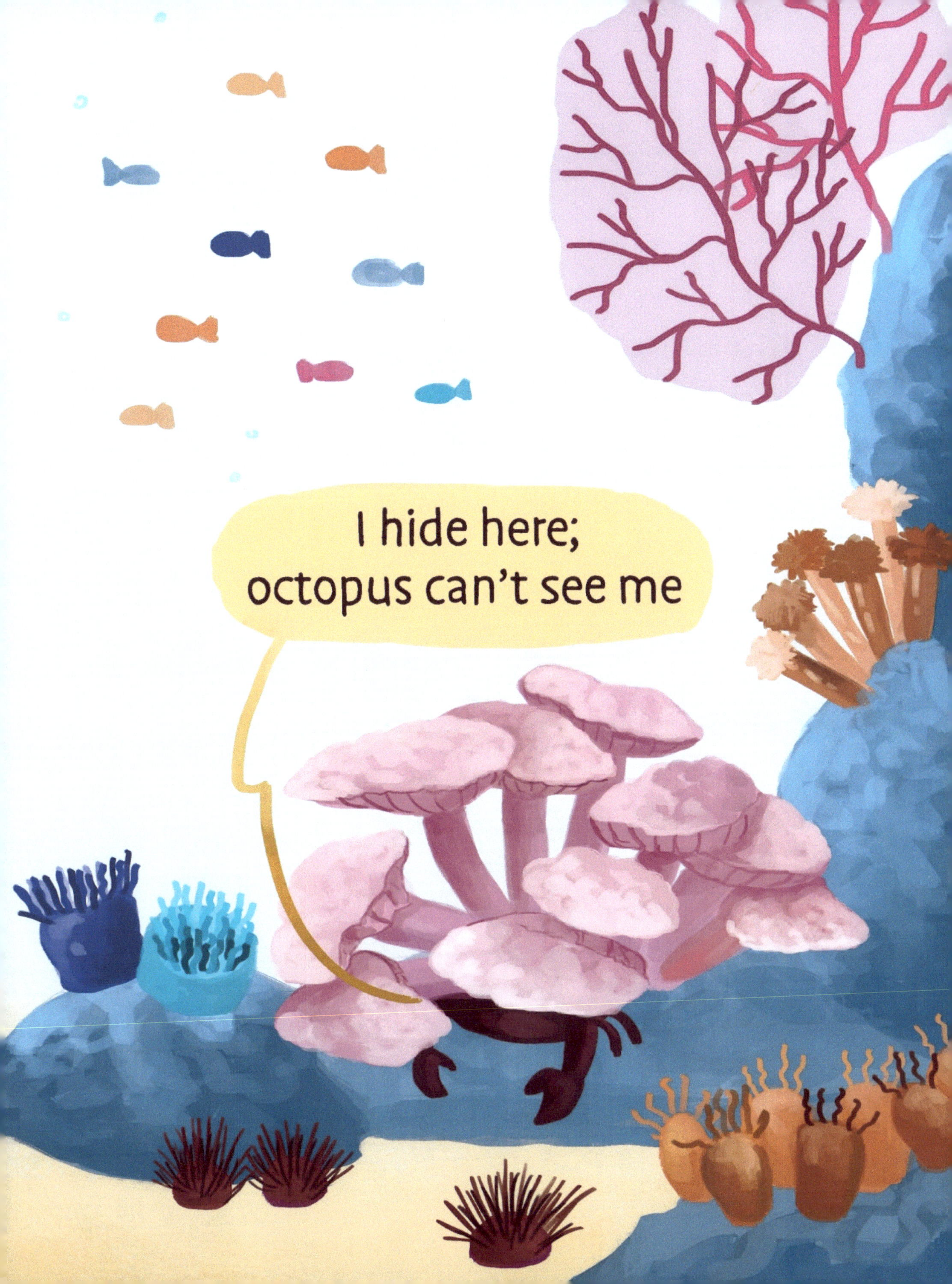
I hide here;
octopus can't see me

Day after day, excitedly, Cartier told his family what he saw under the sea:

- I saw the octopus caught and ate a fish today.

They happily exchanged their experiences with one another. Grandma suggested that Cartier should write a journal of what he saw on his snorkeling trips.

Cartier wrote in his snorkeling journal: "The octopus was shy no more. I saw it caught three fish in a row. Octo shot its tentacle out faster than lightning. It caught and ate a fish – Similar to lizard caught flying insects with its tongue -"

"Mom said that octopi are nocturnal creatures, thus, seeing such was rare. Octopi eat a variety of sea animals."

Days later, Cartier said: - Grandma, Octo caught a crab today.

In his journal, he wrote: "Octopus is very smart! I saw it chased, stalked, and caught a crab today."

leafy sea dragon

weedy sea dragon

Excitedly, Cartier recounted:

- Dad, mom, grandma: Octopus can think! I saw Octo miss a lobster three times last week, and do you know what it did today? Instead of shot tentacle out to snatch the lobster as usual; it crept up the rock behind the lobster, then quietly it dropped down from the top of the rock on the lobster, with all tentacles spread-out like a net. Octo got it! Amazingly smart, don't you think?

pyjama shark

Tears brimming in his eyes, Cartier snuggled against his dad while recounted the shark and the octopus ordeal to his family. - Octo got hurt real bad today. Shark chased it, hunted it. Shark went crazy hunting for Octo among the kelp trees. Very frightening for Octo. It out-smarted the shark, and made it back to its cave; but one tentacle was bitten off by shark. You saw it too, didn't you mom? It might die from its wound.

Cartier visited Octo everyday. It got weaker and weaker. It got so weak to catch food. Afraid that it could die of hunger, with the help of his family, Cartier laid clams, and muscles at the opening of the octopus's cave; in the hope that it would eat them. To his surprise, Octo reached for them from inside the cave. Octo ate them. Cartier fed Octo everyday until it healed.

In his journal, Cartier wrote: "Octo took a month to recover from the shark-bite wound. Its tentacle grew back to the previous size and functioned too."

Cartier wrote in his journal: "Octopus can think and show trust. Octo became friendlier after it recovered from the shark attack. Octo recognized me – It was playing with a school of fish when I arrived. It saw me, it swam toward me – and we played together. I petted it. We are friends now! When I needed to come up for air, it came up with me. We played until time for me to go home."

Journal entry: "Surprised!"

"I saw one more octopus today. Octo has an octopus friend or boy friend or girl friend! I can't tell. 😊"

In the snorkeling journal, few entries later, Cartier wrote: "I didn't see Octo."

"I looked around for it, I swam to its cave. It was there; she was laying eggs. Octo was a girl!" 😊

The last entry in Cartier's snorkeling journal for the year was: "Grandma's said that many fishes die after they lay eggs. I've seen that. I guess, she'd die soon. She's a good life, and good friends. I hope that Octo's babies will be my friends."

THE END

Under The Sea

The Amazing Octopus

By

K.D. Mitchell

Illustrator: Aleksandra Miasmatique

Published by K.D. Mitchell

k.d.mitchell.gg@gmail.com

www.ingramcontent.com/pod-product-compliance
Lightning Source LLC
Chambersburg PA
CBHW041546040426
42447CB00002B/62